INTO THE
ENEMY'S CAMP

By Reverend Brett Connell

ISBN: 978-0-9974541-4-7

Contact the Author
Brett Connell
shiningyourglory@gmx.com

Special thanks to Jesus Christ, Nancy Connell, Evangelist Barbara Lynch, Duncan & Lynda Connell, and Reverend Alan Farkas. Thank you so much for all the support, encouragement, and help in making this book possible.

Reverend Brett Connell attends The Lighthouse Inc. Church of Wyoming, Delaware – Pastored by Evangelist Barbara Lynch.

IN THE BEGINNING
PREFACE

I believe there is a need within the Body of Christ to
not only develop an awareness of spiritual warfare but
to also learn how to engage in this battle between
light and darkness within the scope of God's purpose
for our lives. The real truth is that we are engaged in
battle every day of our lives, even if we don't see or
feel the spiritual pressure. There are so many myths
about the devil, and sadly there aren't enough
churches teaching about sin and the consequences of
evil. Perhaps the most overlooked point is that the
devil is a real enemy, and he desires to destroy us –
because we are precious in God's sight.

Whether we want to believe we are engaged in a
spiritual battle or not, doesn't change its reality and
outcome. We know Jesus came to offer salvation to us
so that we can be reconciled back to God and make

Heaven our home. It is true that God is a God of love and peace, and that He desires and shows mercy. It is also true that God is a God of wrath and judgment, that since the beginning He has purposed to punish evil and the wicked; because He is holy.

Too often we get a mixed message and it is either one or the other. Not enough people are receiving a balanced message of who God is and what He stands for – taking the entirety of the Bible into context. We have an adversary that accuses us before God day and night, one who uses spiritual hosts of wickedness in heavenly places to attack, oppress and bind us so that we cannot freely fulfill the purpose that God has for our lives.

What I hope to convey through this book is the knowledge and understanding of who Lucifer was before he fell from Heaven, and the reason he was found guilty of sin, and why he was cast out of Heaven with one-third of the angels. I want to establish the differences (either in origin or function) between fallen angels, the Watchers from Genesis 6, demons, evil spirits, and ghosts; explaining what their function and purposes are and why we are engaged in a war against them. Lastly, I want to provide the reader with information they can research themselves and come to their conclusions in prayer. I encourage you to pray and invite the Holy Spirit with you as you read, and ask for His truth to be made known to you as you study.

LUCIFER
AND THE FALL

One of the most important parts of war is understanding your enemy. The name, "Lucifer" means 'day star,' or 'son of the morning.' Many recognize it as an alternate name of Satan, the fallen angel. But before his downfall, Lucifer was a magnificent being with a unique ministry.

Lucifer was the original name of Satan. God emphasizes the importance of names, and often changed the names of people throughout the Bible after significant events. Satan (which means the accuser or adversary) is the name he is referenced to after his fall. We will see how Lucifer went from being the praise and worship leader in Heaven and covering the glory of God, to the creature that he has now become, rejected and cast out – doomed to eternal destruction.

Lucifer is one of three archangels mentioned in Scripture (more if you consider the non-canon book of Enoch.) He was created by God just as all angels were, but his role was different from the other angelic hosts. Lucifer was referred to as the 'covering angel.' Just as the cherubim covered the mercy seat of the Ark of the Covenant, Lucifer was established by God to be the angel of worship, one whose ministry surrounded the heart of Heaven. Lucifer was created to dwell eternally in the throne room of Heaven, in the very presence of God.

[Ezekiel 28:14] "You were the anointed cherub who covers; I established you; You were on the holy mountain of God; You walked back and forth in the midst of fiery stones. (NKJV)

We also learn that Lucifer was quite an amazing being to behold:

[Ezekiel 28:12b-13] 12b "You were the seal of perfection, Full of wisdom and perfect in beauty. 13

You were in Eden, the garden of God; Every precious stone was your covering: The sardius, topaz, and diamond, Beryl, onyx, and jasper, Sapphire, turquoise, and emerald with gold. The workmanship of your timbrels and pipes Was prepared for you on the day you were created. (NKJV)

Lucifer was not created begrudgingly. On the very day of his creation, many beautiful instruments were crafted and fashioned just for him. A covering of splendor and glory through many precious gems and stones was made and fitted perfectly to him. This makes you stop and think about the character of an all-knowing God. The great love and care God took to create Lucifer and how He equipped him lavishly, and even called him to the positions in which he held, despite knowing all that would come down the road... that is by definition unconditional love.

Now the context of the previous Scripture is referring to the king of Tyre as he is being addressed about his pride, splendor, and fall. However, it is to the power behind the evil king that this is addressed. The Scripture would not claim that a mortal king in this time period would have dwelled and lived in and among the garden of Eden. The power behind the evil king of Tyre is Satan, which this Scripture is describing. This passage also has a near and far prophecy about Lucifer/Satan because although his end is already certain, it has not happened yet and it occurs after the final judgment (Revelation 20:7-10).

In Ezekiel 28:14 it says, "You were the anointed Cherub." This tells us we are not talking about a human king. The word cherub is singular for cherubim. The cherubim are symbolic of God's Holy presence and His immense glory. These cherubim occupy a unique position. The "anointed cherub who covers" is the picture given to us in the Garden of Eden after Adam and Eve had been sent out and God had placed cherubim to guard the way of the tree of life (Genesis 3:24). Also, when Moses made the mercy seat and placed it into the tabernacle's Holy of Holies, God's glory came and dwelt between the cherubim. They "covered" the mercy seat with their wings (Exodus 25:18-22).

So, we now see that Lucifer was a cherub and his position was to cover the very throne of God with continual praise and worship. Lucifer had the highest of all positions, a position which he eventually despised and lost.

To dwell in the awesome presence of a perfect and holy God, Lucifer had to be perfect. There was nothing ordinary or plain about his appearance. Adorned with gold and precious stones, he truly fit the name, 'Son of the Morning.' He was a step above the other angels, not only in appearance but also in intellect. Lucifer's wisdom far exceeded that of other angelic beings. He understood the ways of God. As the leader of praise and worship, Lucifer had to have a deep understanding of the character and nature of God – to enter into truly deep worship and praise. The word tells us that God is a Spirit, and must be worshiped in spirit and truth.

But Lucifer's splendor and beauty did not last forever. While ministering, he began to consider his position of prominence. Lucifer became prideful, believing that he deserved more than what he already had. He wanted to become like the Most High.

Let's pause here for a moment. While Lucifer was ministering, while he was working for God, he stopped and said these fatal words: "Look at me, and what I did." When we truly praise God, we are centered on Him and acknowledge that all works are His glory and His righteousness. While in true worship, we are humbled before the Almighty Maker. Lucifer had to have *stopped* praising God to consider himself. Once his praise and worship were misdirected and ceased, pride grew uncontrollably within him.

Similarly, when we take our eyes off God and place them upon our circumstances, that is when we begin to entertain and consider the evil thoughts that misdirect our emotions and influence us to make bad decisions contrary to God's word and promises. Let us see now the fall of Lucifer from the heights of Heaven, which resulted in his status as the creature that he is today:

[Isaiah 14:12-14] [12] "How you are fallen from heaven, O Lucifer, son of the morning! How you are cut down to the ground, You who weakened the nations! [13] For you have said in your heart: 'I will ascend into heaven, I will exalt my throne above the stars of God; I will also sit on the mount of the congregation On the farthest sides of the north; [14] I will ascend above the heights of the clouds, I will be like the Most High.' (NKJV)

[Ezekiel 28:15] You were perfect in your ways from the day you were created, Till iniquity was found in you. (NKJV)

This passage goes beyond human history and marks the beginning of sin in the universe and the very fall of Satan in the pristine, sinless spheres before the creation of man. So, what kind of iniquity was found in him? In the book of Ezekiel, God has let us stand with Him at the very beginning, to see the origin and the creation of Lucifer. But, why does God say this? What is this iniquity? We must look back to Isaiah 14:12, which tells us of Lucifer's choice: "I will make myself like the Most High." Did you notice in this passage all of the "I wills"? He said he would exalt his throne above the stars of God. The word "stars" here does not refer to what we see in the night sky. It refers to the angels of God. In other words, "I will take over Heaven, I will be God." That is Lucifer's sin and that is the iniquity that was found in him. He no longer desires to be God's servant. He does not want to do what he was created to do. He wants to be served instead of serving, and millions have chosen to do just that; serve him. They have listened to his lies and chosen to follow him.

Lucifer had wisdom, beauty, ability, perfection, and yet he wanted more; he wanted to be worshiped like

God. But God does not share His glory, nor does He permit another to receive worship. So, before Lucifer had a chance to bring his plan to fruition, he was removed from the presence of God. Cast out of Heaven like a bolt of lightning, Lucifer was stripped of his position and his rights to citizenship in Heaven. Satan's constant attempt ever since has been to oppose the mighty plan of God.

The Bible tells us that Satan took a third of the angels with him. I often wonder how exactly this played out. There had to be a period of time that passed, where God withheld His judgment until the fullness of His purpose was realized. I imagine Satan would have to communicate with and deceive the other angels to even consider rebelling against God with him. Certainly, this was no secret to God, who knows all things – but eventually, a point in time came when the judgment was to be passed.

I have been asked why it is that Satan was not given a chance to repent, and God's character brought into question when it comes to allowing the devil to exist, or why God created him in the first place. I believe the character and nature of God are the foundation of why anything exists at all. If you look back to when Lucifer was created, it was with careful attention and great love. Even knowing beforehand what would happen, God still created him and gave him power and authority. Lucifer had the grace and gifts of God without revocation, free will, and fair opportunity from God despite the inevitable outcome.

The word of God tells us that through every temptation a way of escape is made that we will be able to bear up under it and persevere. Consider this – the grace of God is covering us through temptation, the external force attempting to appeal to our fallen nature to sin.

[1 Corinthians 10:13] No temptation has overtaken you except what is common to mankind. And God is faithful; he will not let you be tempted beyond what you can bear. But when you are tempted, he will also provide a way out so that you can endure it. (NIV)

It is possible that this was ordained to happen in the Master Plan. Lucifer wasn't going to be forgiven of this transgression because of the weighty responsibility he carried along with all the knowledge and wisdom he had. He truly knew better and had to violate his God-given conscience before pondering such an evil thing. Having passed the point of no return with pride, it would be impossible to humble himself to even ask for forgiveness. I also believe that grace did not cover Lucifer because no one tempted him to sin, and it was his own heart that conceived this idea of evil without restraint. That, and he fully intended to bring it to fruition. If you study the mechanics of pride you will see that it produces a hardened heart that cannot be touched – cementing one's actions down a particular path of destruction.

God's nature is to create and love; to give purpose and meaning – to share fellowship and intimacy in relationship with His creation. Sometimes people question God about why evil is allowed to exist, or why certain people were allowed to be born having foreknowledge of the things they have done or would do in their lifetime. The hard truth is that evil has a purpose. Jesus said that offenses must come – and that His purpose was to destroy the works of the devil. Without evil, would there be a need for Salvation? Without a need for dependency on God, would we want Jesus? Would we also be filled with pride eventually?

[Isaiah 54:16] "See, it is I who created the blacksmith who fans the coals into flame and forges a weapon fit for its work. And it is I who have created the destroyer to wreak havoc; (NIV)

God will use evil to fulfill His purposes. If you think about it, *someone* had to betray Jesus. No one would want to do it, but it had to happen to fulfill Scripture. Look what Jesus said:

[John 13:18b] But this is to fulfill this passage of Scripture: 'He who shared my bread has turned against me.' (NIV)

Look back in history – God said plainly in the Bible that He was the one raising up the ruthless Babylonians as an adversary to execute judgment and draw His people closer to Him.

[Habakkuk 1:5-6] [5] "Look at the nations and watch—and be utterly amazed. For I am going to do something in your days that you would not believe, even if you were told. [6] I am raising up the Babylonians, that ruthless and impetuous people, who sweep across the whole earth to seize dwellings not their own. (NIV)

The point here is that God is sovereign. This topic can be explored in depth in my other book, "The Sovereignty of God". His ways are not our ways and rather than accuse God, we should work with what we have (the Word) and live according to its principles. The fact remains that Lucifer fell and became Satan, and works diligently to accomplish the evil that he has planned in his heart.

At this point in the timeline, we have Satan who was thrown down from Heaven along with a third of all the angels with him. Having been stripped of their holy qualities and exiled from their holy estate, having been banished and judged to everlasting torment, they are filled with fury and full of hatred towards God. These beings understand and know the power of God and the reality that their fate is sealed – and their punishment is beyond what they can bear. They were also the first spirits to know what it was to be completely separated from God.

It is from this reality that their hatred and passion to do evil against God was born. One of the main reasons Satan fights us is not because we are that important or powerful; but rather because we are precious to God, and God desires to work through us to accomplish His will – and it is for these reasons

Satan wants to destroy us. Nothing would give Satan more pleasure than bringing as many of God's children to hell with him as he can, to torment the objects of God's affection as spiteful payback for his sin and judgment. Remember, Satan doesn't need to convince us to follow him... only to keep us apart from God.

Satan has been around for all of this world's existence and has had many opportunities to establish footholds within the growth and development of humankind. Satan is the temporary ruler of this world and his demonic hosts work to fulfill his schemes on the earth. This includes invading the sinful nature of mankind and working through human vessels to support and further his evil agendas.

[1 John 5:19] We know that we are children of God, and that the whole world is under the control of the evil one. (NIV)

[Ephesians 6:12] For we do not wrestle against flesh and blood, but against principalities, against powers, against the rulers of the darkness of this age, against spiritual hosts of wickedness in the heavenly places. (NKJV)

Satan, who is the head of this evil world-system is the real, though invisible power behind the successive rulers of Tyre, Babylon, Persia, Greece, Rome, and all of those evil rulers that we have seen come and go in the history of the world. While the kingship or authority of these great empires and nations rested on mere men in positions of power, it was undoubtedly the influence of Satan and his demonic hosts that whispered, and perhaps provoked with temptation, to encourage these men to choose to do the evil things they did.

Satan continues this strategy today. It is the same seats of power and positions of authority, and these are known as thrones and dominions. We can elect new leaders and still see little change – because if

Satan influences a person's heart, the same evil agendas can come forth no matter who the new person is that enters that throne or dominion. That is why we have to engage in spiritual warfare as it pertains to that seat of power or realm of authority. This is why the Bible tells us to engage in warfare against those powers and principalities, the rulers of darkness in heavenly places (the spiritual realms), and not against the flesh and blood vessel.

Up to this point, we have seen Satan with his third of the angels from Heaven, who are now fallen and work together to influence this world system that we live in. This gives us a scope of what is happening spiritually, that there is a spiritual realm we live in and it is infiltrated with fallen angels (demons) following the leadership of their god, Satan. They are at war with God and His holy angels, actively seeking to oppose the Gospel of Jesus Christ – and we are smack dab in the middle of it.

Satan's demonic hosts (the one-third of angels originally from Heaven that fell with him) are the very spiritual forces of wickedness that operate in heavenly places (the spirit realm, but not Heaven itself). These are your powers and principalities of evil and wickedness referenced in the Bible. Just as Heaven has a system of authority, ranks of angels, different types of angels, and a hierarchy, so does Satan and his fallen angels. You will discover that Satan loves to counterfeit and mimic everything that God does in his own evil, twisted way.

ANGELS, HUMAN SPIRITS, AND
THE WATCHERS

I want to show how the angels of God existed before the formation of the world, through a dialogue God is having with Job:

[Job 38:4-7] [4] Where were you when I laid the foundations of the earth? Tell me, if you have understanding. [5] Who determined its measurements? Surely you know! Or who stretched the line upon it? [6] To what were its foundations fastened? Or who laid its cornerstone, [7] when the morning stars sang together, and all the sons of God shouted for joy? (NKJV)

The morning stars sang together, the angels of light, and the sons of God shouting for joy – these are the angelic host. Adam was not made yet, and had no children, so who else would be singing together and shouting for joy during the construction project?

Therefore, men are not what this verse is talking about.

An angel is a spirit being made by God because by Him all things were created. Originally, they were created to worship God and serve Him. While angels are invisible, they have been seen on occasion in the Bible. They also have other purposes since the creation of man, such as holy messengers. Angels coexist in Heaven with human spirits (Hebrews 12:22-24). Though we are like angels we serve a different purpose for God. There are no female angels in Heaven because they are immortal and they do not need to reproduce. However, an angel can come in the form of a woman to appear on earth, because that could be what will minister best to people here in this world, for example, an angelic visitation or a divine encounter that is designed to capture a person's attention.

[Hebrews 13:2] Do not forget to entertain strangers, for by so doing some have unwittingly entertained angels. (NKJV)

It would be silly to think that as we unknowingly entertain angels, that any female we entertain must not or cannot be an angel, according to this Scripture. I firmly believe angels can take the form of male or female vessels to fulfill the purposes of God. The Sadducees came to challenge Jesus asking that if a woman was married seven times, who would be her husband in the resurrection? Jesus answered them:

[Matthew 22:30] For in the resurrection they neither marry nor are given in marriage, but are like angels of God in heaven. (NKJV)

We are all spirit beings created by God in Heaven before the foundation of the world – but we have different assignments, functions, and purposes than angels do. Think of it like this: God created the angels, and us with them. At this point, we are the same. The differences between us came when God purposed different *functions* for each of us. God had decided that some would function as angels, never being physically born but rather serving in Heaven while others would have their spirit placed within a corporeal body and receive the breath of life to become a living soul upon the earth.

Consider this: God created many things within the first six days, as Genesis recounts. There is one important distinction we can make about the process of creation, by which almost everything was created by a command. God spoke and thus it came to be. The Lord, with His authority over all creation, spoke with a word and there was light. He spoke with a word of authority, and the earth was formed – the seas, day and night, it all came to be with a spoken command from the Father of all Lights.

God did not command man and woman to exist in the same way He did with the rest of creation – rather, He lovingly conferred with the Godhead by saying, "Let *us* make man in *our* image, after *our* likeness" (Genesis 1:26a) {Emphasis added}. He then created them male and female and spoke to them about having dominion over the earth and all that was in it (Genesis 1:27-29). Notice how He created them male and female and then had a conversation with them? But wait, I don't remember reading the part yet about God creating man from the dirt and having a lot of time pass while Adam was trying to do stuff, and God concluding that he needed a helper; thus making Eve from his rib…?

Interestingly, that doesn't occur until later in the next chapter. I personally believe that God created our spirits at the beginning with the angels; assigning our personalities, characteristics, attributes, gifts, talents, and abilities. Then later developing the *functions* of male and female – at the time of Genesis 1:26. Our bodies would be fashioned after the image and likeness of God, as would our souls (minds, wills, and emotions). After having made this distinction between angels and soon-to-be humans, God had to conversate with the latter to explain His purpose for us. I believe we see that dialogue in Genesis 1:27-29. In my opinion, I believe we were exactly like the angels in Heaven before the earth was formed because of how the Bible plays this out. (Psalm 139:16)

As humans, we are given a different status than the angels of God. This is another part of the distinction between us. Paul tells us that we will judge angels (1 Corinthians 6:2-3). Angels are not redeemed by Christ (Hebrews 2:16) and the angels are servants to the saints (Hebrews 1:14). This is why I have written in my other books that as part of prayer, we should be utilizing the angels of God to carry out the will of God in our situations and circumstances. By praying to God, we can use our authority in Christ to send angels on assignments to enforce God's desires and His will for our lives and others. As long as our prayers are lined up with the word of God, we should experience many breakthroughs.

Finally, consider this: the Greek word for 'judge' in this Scripture (1 Corinthians 6:2-3) also means 'to rule or govern'. God has already judged the fallen angels – there would be no need for us to do this. The only other angels left are the holy angels, and if they are holy, there is no sin in them for us to judge. Therefore, the inference is "we will rule or govern over the angels" as part of their function to be servants to the saints.

There are, however, another group of angels that had sinned post-rebellion after Lucifer's fall and this would turn out to be one of the greatest turning points in the spiritual realms and how it would drastically affect this world, and that is found in Genesis chapter 6:

[Genesis 6:1-2] [1] Now it came to pass, when men began to multiply on the face of the earth, and daughters were born to them, [2] that the sons of God saw the daughters of men, that they were beautiful;

and they took wives for themselves of all whom they chose. (NKJV)

Humankind was told by God to be fruitful and multiply – this wasn't the problem. The term sons of God in this Scripture refer to angels, and *that* was the problem. Furthermore, men and women produce male or female children; not giants. Supernatural angelic beings, however, provides a different outcome:

[Genesis 6:4] "There were giants on the earth in those days, and also afterward, when the sons of God came in to the daughters of men and they bore children to them. Those were the mighty men who were of old, men of renown." (NKJV)

The word 'giants' here is rendered 'Nephilim' in other translations, because that is the original Greek word that is used.

This is just about the extent the Bible goes into angels having relations with human women and producing offspring. The angels responsible for this are known as 'The Watchers'. There are a few more references to other watchers in the Bible, namely in the book of Daniel. You can find these verses that contain their reference in Daniel chapter 4 verses 13, 17, and 23.

The Watchers that are being discussed in Genesis chapter 6 is the group that chose to be rebellious; they abandoned their assignments and function to participate in sin with human women. The Watchers were angels who were positioned and assigned to oversee the development and progress of mankind. Their rebellion advanced as they continued to multiply with the daughters of men, creating offspring known as the Nephilim. How do we know this? This is a good time to provide a little background on Enoch; who he was, and what he wrote. Let's look at Adam's genealogy from Genesis chapter 5:

[Genesis 5:21-24] 21 Enoch lived sixty-five years, and begot Methuselah. 22 After he begot Methuselah,

Enoch walked with God three hundred years, and had sons and daughters. ^{23} So all the days of Enoch were three hundred and sixty-five years. ^{24} And Enoch walked with God; and he was not, for God took him. (NKJV)

Out of all the family history going back to Adam, Enoch is the only one who was credited as 'walking with God'. Enoch was also the most short-lived out of all of them because God took him. Enoch did not taste death, much the same as Elijah. For someone who only lived 365 years when everyone else is living close to a thousand, and walked with God – and was taken by God into Heaven without experiencing death – I would say that person is highly anointed. Especially since only two people in all creation have had that honor. This is the very same Enoch who is the great-grandfather of Noah, and who also wrote the book of Enoch. The book of Jude quotes Enoch's prophesies, which are written in the book of Enoch, and has many similarities with the Bible.

[Jude 14-15] [14] Now Enoch, the seventh from Adam, prophesied about these men also, saying, "Behold, the Lord comes with ten thousands of His saints, [15] to execute judgment on all, to convict all who are ungodly among them of all their ungodly deeds which they have committed in an ungodly way, and of all the harsh things which ungodly sinners have spoken against Him." (NKJV)

[Enoch 1:9] And behold! He cometh with ten thousands of His holy ones To execute judgement upon all, And to destroy all the ungodly: And to convict all flesh Of all the works of their ungodliness which they have ungodly committed, And of all the hard things which ungodly sinners have spoken against Him.

Many of the first churches and apostles used the book of Enoch in their time, and the book of Enoch is considered canon in the Orthodox Christianity Ethiopian Church.

It is also no surprise that the book of Enoch surfaced again only recently in our time, as stated in the first two verses of the book:

[Enoch 1:1-2] The word of the blessing of Enoch, how he blessed the elect and the righteous, who were to exist in the time of trouble; rejecting all the wicked and ungodly. Enoch, a righteous man, who was with God, answered and spoke, while his eyes were open, and while he saw a holy vision in the heavens. This the angels showed me. From them I heard all things, and understood what I saw; that which will not take place in this generation, but in a generation which is to succeed at a distant period, on account of the elect."

I believe we are part of the end times generation, and that we should practice wisdom and discernment as we glean from Scripture and texts, allowing the Holy Spirit to reveal all truth to us in the proper time and measure. Let's now look at Enoch chapter 6 which ties right in with Genesis chapter 6:

[Genesis 6:4] "There were giants on the earth in those days, and also afterward, when the sons of God came in to the daughters of men and they bore children to them. Those were the mighty men who were of old, men of renown." (NKJV)

[Enoch 6:1-3] [1] And it came to pass, when the sons of men had increased, that in those days there were born to them fair and beautiful daughters. [2] And the Angels, the sons of Heaven, saw them and desired them. And they said to one another: "Come, let us choose for ourselves wives, from the children of men, and let us beget, for ourselves, children."

[Enoch 7:1-6] [1] And they took wives for themselves and everyone chose for himself one each. And they began to go into them and were promiscuous with them. And they taught them charms and spells, and they showed them the cutting of roots and trees. [2] And they became pregnant and bore large giants. And their height was three thousand cubits. [3] These devoured all the toil of men; until men were unable to sustain them. ⁴ And the giants turned against them in order to devour men. ⁵ And they began to sin against birds, and against animals, and against reptiles, and against fish, and they devoured one another's flesh, and drank the blood from it. ⁶ Then the Earth complained about the lawless ones.

This explains that angels of God came down and procreated with human women to breed offspring hybrid giants (known as Nephilim). It is not unheard of that something like this would take place. If you look back to the beginning, a third of the total number of angels in Heaven joined Satan to rebel against God. It wasn't an automatic switch that instantly occurred. Though the Bible doesn't specifically say, it can be deduced that Satan likely deceived some angels through communicative measures as he later did with Eve. If you place yourself in that situation, you can see it would have to take a strong bargain to shift your stance from serving God to Satan. It is reasonable to conclude that this could be achieved by Satan, given his credentials and attributes before his fall.

Secondly, Adam and Eve were in a state of holiness – being covered by God's shekinah glory (not having the realization that they were naked). They lived and communed with God in person, face-to-face. This is further evidence that both angels and humans could either be deceived or tempted into sin, while in a state of holiness. These facts, if you also include Jude's comments on the Watchers (Jude 6), are proof that the direction of a person's choices inevitably has their roots within the condition of their heart. The Watchers did more than just take on the form of fully functional human males and procreate with their human wives that they took for themselves. Let's continue to find out what happened:

[Enoch 8:1-2] [1] And Azazel taught men to make swords, and daggers, and shields, and breastplates. And he showed them the things after these, and the art of making them; bracelets, and ornaments, and the art of making up the eyes, and of beautifying the eyelids, and the most precious stones, and all kinds of colored dyes. And the world was changed. [2] And there was great impiety, and much fornication, and they went astray, and all their ways became corrupt.

While sin was present, it was not gross sin until these angels brought forth their corrupted and supernatural knowledge and introduced it to mankind, wherefore corruption took root and evil entrenched itself into every aspect of human life. It was not beyond their supernatural ability to do such things as they had done thus far, and if one such a being would choose to sin in this capacity, what morals would be in place to stop any further decisions in unrighteousness? The pride of being worshiped by the lesser human counterpart, fulfilling their lusts towards women in the process… such a thing would only bring further corruption and degradation upon the world.

The world would have developed this knowledge in time, independent of outside influence. In other words, the Watchers aren't responsible for all evil in the world since it existed before their influence. The problem was that the world wasn't ready for *all* of that information at one time. This is no different than if you could space travel, with yourself being an advanced race with technology – and coming into contact with a primitive world that had no knowledge of life on other planets. Depending on your moral conduct, you could be seen as a god in that world and very much pollute and destroy its natural course of development if you begin introducing your advanced technological ways to a species that just began development. But the Watchers continued, and did not withhold their forbidden knowledge:

[Enoch 8:3] Amezarak taught all those who cast spells and cut roots, Armaros the release of spells, and Baraqiel astrologers, and Kokabiel portents, and Tamiel taught astrology, and Asradel taught the path of the Moon.

This is why the Bible tells us that such things as sorcery, witchcraft, divination, alchemy, horoscopes, etc. are not holy practices. These are things that were introduced by these angels as they corrupted mankind.

[Deuteronomy 18:10-12a] [10] There shall not be found among you anyone who makes his son or his daughter pass through the fire, or one who practices witchcraft, or a soothsayer, or one who interprets omens, or a sorcerer, [11] or one who conjures spells, or a medium, or a spiritist, or one who calls up the dead. [12a] For all who do these things are an abomination to the Lord (NKJV)

Jude himself speaks of these Watchers, who left their heavenly post of overseeing humankind's development to dwell in the earthly realm cohabiting with women:

[Jude 6] And the angels who did not keep their proper domain, but left their own abode, He has reserved in everlasting chains under darkness for the judgment of the great day; (NKJV)

The Bible does not tell us exactly when Satan was thrown out of Heaven with a third of the angels, but it does say that the Watchers committed their separate rebellion after man was created and had time to reproduce and begin to fill the earth. Therefore, these are two separate events, seeing as how the Watchers held positions of authority after Satan's rebellion with the third of the angels. This is important because Satan and his angels had all their positions and authority revoked upon being thrown out of Heaven. We also know the watcher incident occurred after Satan's rebellion because of the serpent tempting Eve, long before Genesis 6.

Heaven is not full of robot angel-droids that are automatically obedient. God is not a software developer at heart, programming apps to obey codes and functions. God is a loving Father at heart, who gives His creation free will. It pleases God when His creation chooses freely to love Him of their own accord because that is a genuine relationship – and that is what the whole thing is all about. Since this is true, it also allows room for His creation to choose evil as part of their free will. The Bible is filled with examples of both these decisions, for both humans and angels. This is exactly what separates the sheep from the goats – the condition of the heart and the choices that arise from it.

Our story from the beginning is quite an amazing display of God's glory. God knew us all from the *very* beginning and had in His mind every detail of our substance and every day of our lives written down in full detail before even one of them came to be. I believe we were all in spirit-form from the beginning when God created us. Even though the Bible doesn't say *when* God created His holy angels, when studying the Bible in full context I am personally led to believe that God had chosen to create us all together at that undefined point in time – and giving us different functions and assignments as His creativity expanded with the timeline of creation and all things that would follow. Is it feasible to believe that God's creativity is limited to a one-time event, or that His infinite imagination is constrained to a single time frame? Does an artist use only one color? Two colors? Only one portion of the canvas? It strikes me as more likely that God can do as He pleases, with limitless bounds and at any time of His choosing.

[Romans 9:20-21] [20] But who are you, a human being, to talk back to God? "Shall what is formed say to the one who formed it, 'Why did you make me like this?'" [21] Does not the potter have the right to make out of the same lump of clay some pottery for special purposes and some for common use? (NIV)

THE
NEPHILIM

When angels took the form of men with their supernatural abilities and had sexual relations with human women their offspring became giants known as Nephilim. The Nephilim were a product of angelic beings mixed with human DNA; so, the condition of their spirit and soul is a subject for much curiosity.

They weren't fully divine as they were mortal, but they weren't fully human either. Humans have a spirit born of God, and a soul (mind, will, and emotions) breathed into them from God. The Nephilim are different in the context that their spirit was not directly born of God, but rather a mere product of their supernatural fathers (the fallen Watchers). Yes, God created all things and all things belong to Him (Hebrews 2:10) – but it is the same situation as the following analogy:

Think about it in this way: if mankind developed enough in advanced technology, and was able to create an artificial intelligence (AI) that became self-aware that it was 'alive', as a sentient lifeform by definition, capable of learning and growing on its own, and then that same AI turned around and created an artificial lifeform of its own (an android, for example) who would the creator be of the second-generation android? Would it be the man responsible for inventing the technology, or the AI who chose to create it? The short answer is that the sentient AI is directly responsible for the second-generation android, but it would require the intervention of the human responsible for the technology to *govern* their existence since man is ultimately *accountable* for both the first- and second-generation androids.

Similarly, the Watchers were directly responsible for creating the Nephilim, but it would require God's intervention to govern them and their actions (they still fall under God's sovereignty and dominion, belonging to Him). While the Nephilim are not born of God's true Spirit, and hence have no dwelling in Heaven, God still has full sovereignty over them and the power to judge them. Sin and degradation proceeded through the Nephilim until all the world was corrupted. This is where we see the parallel between Genesis 6 and Enoch 8:

[Genesis 6:11-12] [11] The earth also was corrupt before God, and the earth was filled with violence. [12] So God looked upon the earth, and indeed it was corrupt; for all flesh had corrupted their way on the earth. (NKJV)

[Enoch 8:2] And there was great impiety, and much fornication, and they went astray, and all their ways became corrupt.

I personally feel as though this is one of the reasons why God established a holy ordinance concerning the priests who served and represented Him. If you look at Leviticus 21:1-15 you will see that God had forbidden the priests to marry impure women. There are some other regulations also as far as safeguarding the priests from unholy contact and interaction with wives and women that would cause defilement. Such commandments would serve to protect the priests and teach holy boundaries that would seek to prevent sins committed in the past.

In Enoch chapter 9 it tells us that Michael, Gabriel, Suriel, and Uriel looked down upon the earth and saw all the evil continually taking place. They immediately went before God and sought counsel with what should be done:

[Enoch 9:6-8] [6] See then what Azazel has done; how he has taught all iniquity on the earth and revealed the eternal secrets that are made in Heaven. [7] And Semyaza has made known spells, he to whom you gave authority to rule over those who are with him. [8] And they went into the daughters of men together, lay with those women, became unclean, and revealed to them these sins.

So, let's rewind and see what happened.

The Watchers were angels that were likely given assignments that pertained to humankind upon the earth. They became enamored with the daughters of men and then married and reproduced with them. These angels of God are the ones referred to in Jude 1:6 "And the angels who did not keep their proper domain, but left their own abode, He has reserved in everlasting chains under darkness for the judgment of the great day;"

They came down from their heavenly places and into the world to appear as men – and had relations with women, and had children with them. Their children were numerous and many and were also giants. These Nephilim giants were not born of the Spirit of God – but rather a byproduct of the Watchers through mortal women. What does it mean to not be born of the Spirit of God?

[Enoch 15:8] Now the giants, who have been born of spirit and of flesh, shall be called upon earth evil spirits, and on earth shall be their habitation. Evil spirits shall proceed from their flesh, because they were created from above; from the holy watchers was their beginning and primary foundation. Evil spirits shall they be upon the earth, and the spirits of the wicked shall they be called. The habitation of the spirits of heaven shall be in heaven; but upon the earth shall be the habitation of terrestrial spirits, who are born on earth.

Again, this proves to us that God Himself did not directly place the spirit-bodies of the Nephilim within them, as though they were of Him, but rather allowed this byproduct to exist and develop between spirit-bodied Watchers and human women. Think back to our analogy of the sentient artificial intelligence creating a second-generation android. The spirit-bodies were a knock-off from an angelic being. While they (the Nephilim) were not supernatural beings, they had enhanced physical capabilities. These people, these giants, had no hope of making Heaven their home. An angel cannot be redeemed and saved, and neither can their offspring born through rebellion towards God and in sin. This is why Enoch pointed out "the giants, who have been born of spirit and of flesh" rather than saying "sons of God," or "born of His Spirit".

Also note that as Enoch makes that distinction, he goes right into the fact that these Nephilim are literally to be called evil spirits upon the earth – and earth will be their only habitation. Furthermore, Enoch continues to say when the Nephilim die, evil spirits will proceed from their flesh. Why? Because they were created from above (the supernatural realm) *from the holy Watchers* (their beginning and primary foundation) and not from God Himself. Think about it in human terms for the sake of understanding the principle: would you service and honor a warranty for a product that wasn't even yours?

The book of Enoch explains to us that evil spirits fully comprise the makeup of the Nephilim and that when they die, they will release those multitudes of evil spirits upon the earth. It is those evil spirits that will be confined to the earth with the function and purpose of bruising, oppressing, tormenting, and resisting humankind. Elsewhere in this book it even uses phrasing and terminology to describe that these evil spirits do not eat nor drink, and cannot have any rest or peace. This is very similar to when Jesus explained what happens when an evil (unclean) spirit is cast out of a person in Matthew 12:43.

If you read the book of Enoch in further detail, it illustrates exactly how God handled and judged these things in detail. Evil and wickedness proceeded upon all the earth, and all who were in it, and God bound these angels (the Watchers) in everlasting chains to always remain under darkness until the final day. The flood came, Noah and his family were spared, and the timeline continued. Let's pause for a moment here and consider something that took place around this point in the timeline:

Now here's an interesting fact… the Bible tells us in Genesis 6:4 "There were giants on the earth in those days, and also afterward …" This implies that even after the flood, after the days of Noah, there were Nephilim giants on the earth. But how could this be? If God destroyed the wickedness in the earth but spared only Noah and his family, how could Nephilim be allowed to continue to exist? We will answer these questions shortly.

God spared Noah and his family because he (Noah) was righteous among that generation. This does not strictly imply that his entire family was also righteous of their own merits or actions. It could be that because Noah was righteous, God spared his family also, even if they were not righteous. But the Bible does not specifically declare Noah's family to be evil, either. To draw our conclusion here, we have to default to the character of God. God desires that none should perish, but that all would come to repentance (2 Peter 3:9). In other words, God desires mercy rather than sacrifice (Matthew 9:13). God also had recently given mankind the command "be fruitful and multiply, fill the earth and subdue it" (Genesis 1:28) and therefore it would be detrimental to God's desire, and His command given, to stop the progression of human life and development. This is exactly what would happen if He had spared Noah only. So, to fulfill Scripture and His divine purposes, God chose to spare Noah's family also, so that his sons and daughters-in-law could continue to multiply upon the earth. It was not so much about whether or not Noah's family members were righteous and worthy to be spared – but more about the long-term purposes God had in mind.

Assuming we're taking the route of belief that all life was wiped out in the flood except Noah, his family, and the animals on the boat we need to explore a little about how genetics work. Genetics are adaptable and can change over the course of generations – science has proven this. A person's genes can change and adapt within themselves and be in a different state when being passed down to the next generation, this is something called epigenetic modification. Genes are carriers of information, DNA contains code and instructions for how to develop and even contains traits, characteristics, and features of who and what we are. Our genetic coding is something we inherit from our parents and something we pass down to our children. You may be aware that certain illnesses, disorders, and diseases can be passed down from one generation to another because of that information being contained within the DNA. Just because you may have some anomaly in your DNA doesn't mean you've done anything wrong – you were never in control of your genes, to begin with.

No one knows exactly how Nephilim DNA survived the flood and was able to manifest itself in the days afterward. There are several schools of thought: It is possible that Noah's family could have been carriers in part, of Nephilim DNA. Through no fault of their own, it is possible their genes could have carried that genetic coding. The Bible also does not specify whether or not any of Noah's daughters-in-law were pregnant before they came onto the boat. Having just come out of the world's biggest nightmare of genetic pollution and disaster, to the point God had to kill off the entire planet, it would stand to reason that some remnant of those evil byproducts could at some level be reflected in their DNA. Remember, DNA and genetics are long-term changes, not short-term. A freight train moving at 50mph doesn't just instantly stop – it takes roughly a mile to come to a complete stop, and like genetics, the things developed there take time to be worked out through the generations. Another speculated belief held by others is that perhaps some Nephilim had hidden underground during the flood, preserving their DNA to resurface post-flood. Regardless of how it managed to survive at least in part after the flood, the Scripture reveals to us that the giants were in the lands and that the descendants of Anak were Nephilim.

According to the science of genetics, the DNA and chromosomes halved in the contribution of 2 parents have to match closely to be able to combine. This means the DNA and chromosomes of the angels who appeared as men would have to be almost identical to real human DNA. For example, a chimpanzee's DNA is estimated to be about 95% similar to human DNA, and chimpanzees have 24 chromosomes while humans have 23. The differences are only a matter of 1 chromosome and 5% of the DNA, yet the bodies of humans and chimpanzees are vastly different and are incapable of intermixing.

Therefore, the angels appearing as men would have to have DNA that is even more closely matched to human women, although it wouldn't be exactly matched. You would certainly not have pure human DNA. You would have hybrid DNA. This illegal transaction that took place between angels and women corrupted the DNA of mankind. These genetic mutations caused, in part, the giantism gene, among many other various forms of mutations such as having six appendages. Just look at Goliath, a Philistine who was a giant. Also, look at King Og of Bashan who was about 14 feet tall (his bed was 9 cubits long according to Deuteronomy 3:11).

God speaks directly to these angels and their human wives and tells them, "And the Lord said, "My Spirit shall not strive with man forever, for he is indeed flesh; yet his days shall be one hundred and twenty years." (Genesis 6:3). The verse of God's judgment of shortened life-spans is placed in between the verse describing these angels taking wives and having sex with them, and the verse telling of their giant children, the Nephilim, who committed every evil act and destroyed man and each other.

We see remnants of evil giants after the flood – a few of them we mentioned earlier. Perhaps most notably, when the Israelites were sent out to spy the land one of the first things some of them reported was the fear of the giants in those lands:

[Numbers 13:32b-33] [32b] They said, "The land we explored is one that devours those who live there. All the people we saw there are very tall. [33] We saw Nephilim there. (The descendants of Anak are Nephilim.) We felt as small as grasshoppers, and that's how we must have looked to them." (GW)

One of Satan's strategies was to corrupt man's DNA so badly that the Messiah may not be born among men through a pure line of David (Matthew 1:1) Obviously, this strategy failed, but this gives us all insight into the battles taking place spiritually.

[Enoch 12:5-7] "Then the Lord said to me: Enoch, scribe of righteousness, go tell the Watchers of heaven, who have deserted the lofty sky, and their holy everlasting station, who have been polluted with women. And have done as the sons of men do, by taking to themselves wives, and who have been greatly corrupted on the earth; That on the earth they shall never obtain peace and remission of sin. For they shall not rejoice in their offspring; they shall behold the slaughter of their beloved; shall lament for the destruction of their sons; and shall petition for ever; but shall not obtain mercy and peace."

This is fulfilled in the Bible not only by the destructive nature of the pre-flood Nephilim but also by the flood itself – and even after, God using the Israelites (His chosen people) to kill the godless nations that were to be eliminated (including the descendants of Anak) and to possess their land. The Watchers who originally abandoned their dwelling in Heaven were bound in darkness under the earth until the final day of Judgment. Hence, there are no known pure Nephilim roaming the earth today.

EVIL SPIRITS, DEMONS, AND
THE FALLEN ANGELS

The Bible has a lot to say about demons, which are considered evil (or unclean) spirits. Firstly, I want to establish upfront here that fallen angels and demons are in essence the same thing – in the context that they are spirit beings that were never fully or exclusively human. Both of these spiritual beings rebelled against God's laws and were judged accordingly. Either they fell because of rebellion or were a byproduct of its consequences. The Bible tells us that when Lucifer sinned and lost his authority in Heaven, that he took with him one-third of the angels before being cast out of his original dwelling place:

[Revelation 12:3-4] [3] And another sign appeared in heaven: behold, a great, fiery red dragon having seven heads and ten horns, and seven diadems on his heads. [4] His tail drew a third of the stars of heaven and threw them to the earth. And the dragon stood before the woman who was ready to give birth, to devour her Child as soon as it was born. (NKJV)

This is Satan taking with him a third of the angels, to form his own army in an attempt to destroy the Root of David, Jesus Christ as He was born into the world. You can see this spiritual side of battle being explained in Revelation, but you can also read about the physical manifestation of this taking place in Jesus' early years through king Herod when (the evil influence of Satan) convinced him to order every male child 2 years old and under to be killed to prevent Jesus from fulfilling His role as King (Matthew 2:13-18).

[Revelation 12:8-9] [8] but they did not prevail, nor was a place found for them in heaven any longer. [9] So the great dragon was cast out, that serpent of old, called the Devil and Satan, who deceives the whole world; he was cast to the earth, and his angels were cast out with him. (NKJV)

This one-third of the angels in Heaven chose by some undetermined reason to follow Satan and become subject to his rulership. As a result, they have become fallen angels that share in Satan's judgment – but are allowed to operate within the spheres of this world and the heavenly places, but not Heaven itself. These fallen angels are in essence demons, in the context that they were once angels of God, but have sinned and are now fully demonic. These are your evil powers, principalities, and rulers of wickedness in heavenly places.

[Ephesians 6:12] For we do not wrestle against flesh and blood, but against principalities, against powers, against the rulers of the darkness of this age, against spiritual hosts of wickedness in the heavenly places. (NKJV)

Satan is the prince of this world, and ruler over the powers of the air, governing the fallen angels that operate with their wickedness in the heavenly places

(Ephesians 2:1-2). He also has limited power and authority over the whole world and can exercise his influence over everyone in it (1 John 5:19). The Bible tells us through a dialogue Satan is having with Jesus, that God has (in His sovereignty) given this authority to Satan (Luke 4:6). Jesus didn't respond to the devil calling out any bluff or lie; because He knew Satan usurped Adam's authority in the Garden through sin – but rather rebuked the part of that dialogue where Satan wanted Jesus to worship him (for it).

One of Satan's titles is the "prince of demons" (Matthew 9:34) and he has his kingdom by which he rules over all evil spirits (Matthew 12:26). Furthermore, he has his throne set up in the world (Revelation 2:13). This is why the Bible tells us that at the appointed time, God will visit and punish the hosts of heaven (the powers and principalities of the air) for their evil conduct, as well as their human counterparts on earth (the kings and rulers of nations) that yielded their vessels to their influence for evil purposes:

[Isaiah 24:21] And in that day the Lord will visit and punish the host of the high ones on high [the host of heaven in heaven, celestial beings] and the kings of the earth on the earth. (AMPC)

We had said earlier that Satan mimics what God does in His kingdom of Light. Often an antichrist spirit will try to imitate the genuine Holy Spirit in many kinds of manifestations while performing many false signs, wonders, and miracles. Again, the purpose of all of this is to attempt to deceive as many as possible to steer them away from the truth. Remember, Satan doesn't have to convince people to exclusively follow him – only to steer them away from Christ which is their hope of Salvation.

Satan has a hierarchy in his demonic kingdom. There are top-level demons that have high ranks with entire legions under their command. This type of system works its way down until you have all the lesser demons at the bottom that perform their own evil assignments and are being told what to do and where to go by others above them.

Regarding the fallen angels that rebelled with Satan, their primary function and general positions are to govern and oversee larger-scale tactical efforts being made within the kingdom of darkness. These are most often the powers and principalities that have authority over entire states, regions, and even countries. Fallen angels *are* demons in every sense of the term and they are not limited to operating in heavenly places. The Bible tells us they were hurled down to the earth with Satan, and therefore these demons are entirely capable of operating from any location in various capacities. Again, only one condition matters to Satan and his demonic host: The human spirit must not make contact with the Holy Spirit of God. As long as this result is achieved, any means or method is acceptable.

Let's contrast these fallen angels and their origin with what the book of Enoch tells us about the evil spirits (demons) that originated from the Nephilim. These evil spirits had no part in Heaven and were condemned to roam this world with the very purpose and function to bruise, oppress, torment, and afflict mankind. These are the ones that thirst and hunger but cannot find peace or rest. They are subject to the authority of the prince of this world, and the fallen angels that govern the heavenly places above this world in their wickedness, receiving their orders from Satan.

[Enoch 15:11] And the spirits of the giants afflict, oppress, destroy, attack, do battle, and work destruction on the earth, and cause trouble: they take no food, (but nevertheless hunger) and thirst, and cause offences. And these spirits shall rise up against the children of men and against the women, because they have proceeded (from them).

Fallen angels rebelled against God in Heaven and were thus kicked out with Satan. They *were* holy angels at one point. This is what distinguishes them from lesser demons that are bound to the earth because of the sinful acts of the Watchers and the Nephilim. These evil spirits were never part of Heaven. The Watchers are of the same origin as fallen angels, with the only difference being that they were not part of the *original* rebellion. Remember, Satan had rebelled before the Garden – and the Watchers rebelled in Genesis 6.

A lot of what you may hear is a simple matter of terminology. If you want to simplify the differences between these categories you can say that fallen angels, demons, and the Watchers are all the same in the context they are evil and have had a judgment pronounced upon them. They all have the same function – to destroy the plans and purposes of God through mankind. You can differentiate these three categories by studying *how* they do that. Oftentimes the upper echelon tiers of demons are your fallen angels – typically they are the present-day powers and principalities of wickedness in heavenly places, while the demons being cast out of people are at times the lesser demons that are bound to this earth as Enoch mentions. Is it possible that Satan could direct an original fallen angel by having it roam the earth possessing people doing the same thing as a lowly demon? Absolutely. I personally believe that the nature of Satan is total evil in its purest form – and so long as a demon has a legal right to enter into and possess a person or otherwise afflict, torment, and oppress them; then it doesn't matter if it's the lowest rank or the highest. Once again, as long as the end justifies the means – he will do it.

Also, consider where we are on the timeline of events. As we get closer to the end times, the darkness will get stronger. This includes the demons' activity over people that are bound by sin and curses. As the end draws nearer, we're going to see higher-level demonic activity coming out of the woodwork. Think of it like this: Satan's strategy for hundreds of years has been to deny his existence. The more he remained hidden the better, and it allowed him to make light of any subject of the devil or his evil schemes. The seriousness of his battlefield has been reduced to cartoonish humor and gave him the edge he needed against the church. But there is coming a time when Satan will be right out in the open, and he will no longer desire to be hidden but rather openly worshiped by everyone. For biblical prophecy to be fulfilled there will require great darkness to cover the land and be saturated in all societies. It is going to take upper-echelon demons higher up the ranks to accomplish many of the assignments needed to bring this about, including possession by fallen angels and lesser demons alike.

I will say this though, in my years of ministry I have seen some very astounding and even bizarre things when it comes to the demonic activity we have witnessed. I know that the forces of evil will do whatever it takes to lead a soul away from Christ, quite literally by any means necessary. Many deliverance ministers or anyone who has a moderate knowledge of spiritual warfare can tell you that there are countless types of demons with many functions and seemingly endless assignments over people. One thing that stands out for sure is that Satan tries to imitate and mimic everything God does. While he doesn't have anything original of his own, he sure does love to copy whatever God is doing. For example, God has a kingdom and a throne, and so does Satan. God works through His people to accomplish His will – and so does the enemy. God protects His chosen ones, and so does the devil. Heaven has a hierarchy and system of authority and rulership, and so does the devil.

Then now consider this, but strap on your seatbelt and put on your helmet so your belief doesn't go flying: Is it possible that demons, supernatural beings, could appear as men – as angels do? We know that Satan and his demons can appear as an angel of light, so why wouldn't they employ this tactic? Whether appearing as a humanoid or simply manifesting within the soul of an individual, the devil, and his evil hosts can carry out their assignments through and against mankind.

The underlings and demons that roam the earth are not without significance, however. They play a key role in bringing about the many plans of Satan for this world, before the judgment of God spelled out in the Word takes place. We still have some time before the second coming of Jesus, and it is going to get incredibly dark before it's all said and done. The evil spirits we often encounter without even realizing it still have an ordained time period to operate here on the earth. If you look at the Bible and Revelation, there are still dark times and events that must yet take place. The divine timeline provides the demons more time to operate. Listen to what the demons said to Jesus when being confronted within the man at Gadarenes:

[Mark 5:10] And he kept begging Him urgently not to send them [himself and the other demons] away out of that region. (AMPC)

The unclean spirits here that originated from the offspring of the Watchers were judged and sentenced to be bound to the earth. At the very least, these unclean spirits would desire more than anything to stay within the region they were familiar with. That is one of the few things they probably had any control over, if possible. Also, we have seen territorial disputes between spirits take place – power struggles and displays of dominance and intimidation between two groups of demons from different regions. Satan's kingdom is ruled by pride, hatred, evil, and violence. I believe this is why the demons begged not to be cast out of the region – whereby they would be forced to integrate themselves with other territorial spirits. Remember, the Nephilim were evil from the beginning – destroying all that man had produced until the earth could no longer sustain them – and they eventually turned on each other in a giant demonic blood bath. Surely this infighting and bitterness would spill over to their spiritual lifespan after their flesh had been destroyed?

The principle of demonic hosts in heavenly places seeking power and influence over particular regions and territories is found in the Bible during the spiritual battle involving Daniel and his prayer to God:

[Daniel 10:12-13] [12] Then he said to me, "Do not fear, Daniel, for from the first day that you set your heart to understand, and to humble yourself before your God, your words were heard; and I have come because of your words. [13] But the prince of the kingdom of Persia withstood me twenty-one days; and behold, Michael, one of the chief princes, came to help me, for I had been left alone there with the kings of Persia. (NKJV)

Principalities that control regions have assignments and responsibilities. It is up to them to ensure that their area is dominated by sin and under the control of Satan. They must actively seek and pursue to stop any plan or activity of God that aims to liberate the demonic hold over that region. Oftentimes, God will use human vessels equipped to do this work – but at times, a sovereign move of God is performed to sway the balance of power and shift the spiritual atmosphere through the principle of blessings and curses.

There are times that it seems like God isn't answering our prayers and we may begin to waiver or lose hope in times of desperation. But if we look here at this Scripture, it is possible that we could be in the same situation as Daniel was. The moment you went before God and started praying, you were immediately heard – and the answer to that prayer was dispatched. Yet, could it be possible that your answer is being held up by the princes of the air? Perhaps you should pray to God, asking Him to release chief angels equipped to loosen the hold upon the delivery of your answer? Just some food for thought.

The unclean spirits are going to be here as long as humankind is upon the earth. The only exception is during the thousand-year reign when the devil is temporarily locked up in the pit – until he is released for a short time, and soon after judged with every other unrighteous thing that has taken place. That will be the end of the story that was written so far.

THE NEPHILIM
RETURN

Before we get too excited, I want to reinforce what I had said earlier that the Watchers are not going to come out of their prisons to recreate their sins from the past. We need to first look at some things the Bible says about the future days to see where this is going. We also need to look at current events to gauge where we are at in biblical prophecy. Once we get a handle on where we are and *when* we are in the biblical timeline, we should have a decent starting point to explain how this ancient evil is going to be conjured up in the last days.

The Bible gives us insight as to how things will generally unfold in the end times. Things are getting darker, and as you have probably noticed morality has been weakening over the last several decades, and society as a whole has grown more accustomed to sin and evil. The very ideals and acts that are portrayed and committed today would have been unacceptable even just 50 years ago, to the point of the proverbial 'mob and pitch fork' crowd driving out the offenders.

The disciples asked Jesus what signs to look out for that would foretell His Second Coming (Matthew 24). In these descriptions, Jesus is saying that they (believers in Christ) will be hated by all nations because of Him; that they will be delivered up to tribulation (persecution, distress, confinement) and killed. This already happens in many parts of the world and you are starting to see it here in America. If you try to confront many of the socially acceptable practices in today's world with what the Bible clearly says about such actions, defining them as sin, you will be arrested, jailed, hated, mocked, and labeled. The Bible says in the last days that people will call good evil and evil good. This is exactly what is taking place and will continue to develop at its deepest levels.

[Matthew 24:21-22] [21] For at that time there will be a great tribulation (pressure, distress, oppression), such as has not occurred since the beginning of the world until now, nor ever will [again]. 22 And if those days [of tribulation] had not been cut short, no human life would be saved; but for the sake of the elect (God's chosen ones) those days will be shortened. (AMP)

Let's compare what Joel and Revelation share in common about "The Day of the Lord" in the end times:

[Joel 2:1-11] 1 Blow the trumpet in Zion [warning of impending judgment], Sound an alarm on My holy mountain [Zion]! Let all the inhabitants of the land tremble and shudder in fear, For the [judgment] day of the Lord is coming; It is close at hand, 2 A day of darkness and gloom, A day of clouds and of thick [dark] mist, Like the dawn spread over the mountains; There is a [pagan, hostile] people numerous and mighty, The like of which has never been before Nor will be again afterward Even for years of many generations. 3 Before them a fire

devours, And behind them a flame burns; Before
them the land is like the Garden of Eden, But behind
them a desolate wilderness; And nothing at all
escapes them. [4] Their appearance is like the
appearance of horses, And they run like war horses. [5]
Like the noise of chariots They leap on the tops of
the mountains, Like the crackling of a flame of fire
devouring the stubble, Like a mighty people set in
battle formation. [6] Before them the people are in
anguish; All faces become pale [with terror].

[7] They run like warriors; They climb the wall like
soldiers. They each march [straight ahead] in line,
And they do not deviate from their paths. [8] They do
not crowd each other; Each one marches in his path.
When they burst through the defenses (weapons),
They do not break ranks. [9] They rush over the city,
They run on the wall; They climb up into the houses,
They enter at the windows like a thief. [10] The earth
quakes before them, The heavens tremble, The sun
and the moon grow dark And the stars lose their
brightness. [11] The Lord utters His voice before His

army, For His camp is very great, Because strong and powerful is he who [obediently] carries out His word. For the day of the Lord is indeed great and very terrible [causing dread]; Who can endure it? (AMP)

These passages explain to us that there is going to be an end-time army that is raised up by, and used by, God – to destroy. Now hold on before some of the religious folk go supernova... this is only happening because it is a *judgment* from God. Look what God says:

[Isaiah 54:16] "See, it is I who created the blacksmith who fans the coals into flame and forges a weapon fit for its work. And it is I who have created the destroyer to wreak havoc; (NIV)

This isn't God's first rodeo, either. In times past, He has done the very same thing:

[Habakkuk 1:5-6] 5 "Look at the nations and watch— and be utterly amazed. For I am going to do something in your days that you would not believe, even if you were told. ⁶ I am raising up the Babylonians, that ruthless and impetuous people, who sweep across the whole earth to seize dwellings not their own. (NIV)

But let's go back and look closely at verses 4-5 of Joel chapter 2:

[Joel 2:4-5] ⁴ Their appearance is like the appearance of horses, And they run like war horses. ⁵ Like the noise of chariots They leap on the tops of the mountains, Like the crackling of a flame of fire devouring the stubble, Like a mighty people set in battle formation. (AMP)

This is reflected in a different account of the end time horrors that will be unleashed upon the earth:

[Revelation 9:7-8] ⁷ The locusts resembled horses prepared and equipped for battle; and on their heads appeared to be [something like] golden crowns, and their faces resembled human faces. [8] They had hair like the hair of women, and their teeth were like the teeth of lions. (AMP)

Let's pause for a moment and play a little imagination game. Imagine being alive roughly 2,000 years ago and the only things you know of are what you have seen in your present time. Let's assume a higher power opens a portal and shows you visions of what is taking place in this world over 2 millennia into the future. Obviously, there have been some advancements in technology, and we've even seen skits on TV like this where someone got zapped into the future or the entire plot takes place in the distant future. Chances are, you aren't going to be able to describe very well the things you're seeing right away – because you only have knowledge and reference to the things you presently know. For example, trying to describe an automobile made in 2021 from someone who lives in 90 A.D. would probably only be able to describe it as a horseless chariot with steel armor and blazing light coming out of its eyes that blinded men who looked upon it (those LED headlights) with the sound of a thousand horses charging into battle (the engine noise). It has wings that open up (doors), etc. They might even say the thing was a giant locust if they saw a helicopter.

So, it's hard to fully understand exactly what these writers and recipients of these visions had truly seen, but using this effect we can be open to interpretation within reasonable limits. The Bible is referring to a very powerful and seemingly unstoppable army that is going to strike abject terror into the hearts of men and people's faces will drain of color in total despair and not one will be spared. It would seem as though no one could stop this army, as they are so unified together and march towards their objectives without fail or hindrance – almost as though they were *engineered* or *programmed* to do so.

Imagine an army of soldiers the likes of which has never been seen before, and will never be seen again, according to the Scriptures? This is literally a one-time army of the wildest, nightmare proportions. Anything we have right now does not compare to it, and we have some pretty nasty stuff on this planet including some top-secret government projects, I would imagine. So how does all this plug into our timeline? Let's insert our hinging Scripture that is going to join together the former and latter topics:

[Matthew 24:37] But as the days of Noah were, so also will the coming of the Son of Man be. (NKJV)

What was going on in the days of Noah? Well besides the fact that everyone was just doing their own thing while total doom and destruction were setting in and everyone besides Noah and his family died as a result. We have to look back further as to the reason *why* the judgment was passed on the earth to destroy every living thing on it.

There was total evil in every heart and all anyone cared about was acting out that perverse evil continually. Remember the Watchers? They became enamored with lustful thoughts and intents and mixed their seed with human women, producing the Nephilim. The Nephilim were giants, mighty men of war – renowned warriors that destroyed everything in sight until mankind nor the earth itself could accommodate them any longer. The souls of men, their blood, the earth itself, like Abel, cried out from the ground unto the gates of Heaven for justice. God was then grieved and was sorry that he made man, and judged all earth's inhabitants minus Noah and his family because Noah had favor in God's eyes as a righteous man.

It could be said that the DNA of mankind was nearly completely corrupted at this point and a hard reset was needed. So where does the devil come into play here?

Firstly, we know that the devil loves to counterfeit whatever God is doing. He is so full of pride that he is blinded by it. He so desperately wants to be like the Most High, that he won't settle for anything less than the best emulation of God's ways in his own twisted, evil power. Take for example the very way in which God brought forth His Son Jesus into the world. Mary was impregnated by the Holy Spirit as she was still a virgin. God used a human vessel (Mary's womb) to follow the procedure of normal human development. Think about the physical aspect of this. I believe fully in the power of miracles – divine intervention, and the fact that God has the power to literally snap His fingers and turn the entire multiverse upside down. But I also understand that God uses the very things He created; math, science, physics, quantum mechanics, etc. to accomplish and fulfill His purposes.

Some of us know that to create human life, you need two pairs of DNA. That DNA needs to be very closely matched to join together and replicate into a lifeform. In other words, a chimpanzee cannot mate with a horse and expect to produce offspring – their DNA is not compatible. As we said earlier, humans and chimpanzee's DNA only differ by less than 5%

yet it is completely incompatible with one another. So, the Holy Spirit had to have created the DNA that would be used to form Jesus' human body within Mary's womb. God did not use a male vessel nor an angelic form to come into Mary, as such a thing would be no different than what the Watchers did. This was different. This conception of Jesus was holy and pure.

Since Jesus' DNA of his human body was pure, holy, and made by the Holy Spirit – He was born without sin. Joseph's personal and generational sins did not pass down, because Jesus did not come from Joseph but the Holy Spirit. Having said that, we need to look at the latter days when Satan is going to manifest his agents into this world. Something interesting takes place in Genesis when God places enmity between the serpent and the woman:

[Genesis 3:15] "And I will put enmity (open hostility) between you and the woman, and between your seed (offspring) and her Seed; He shall [fatally] bruise your head, and you shall [only] bruise His heel." (AMP)

There are several things to note here. Firstly, the "Seed" of the woman is capitalized, and references to "Him" (the Seed of the woman) are also capitalized. These are references to Jesus, which would come through the woman's seed in David's line to fatally crush Satan's head under His feet. Secondly, this verse tells us that the serpent (Satan) has a seed that can produce offspring. The Greek word used here for seed is 'zera'. [Strongs 2233] It means literally 'children, descendants, posterity'. This same Greek word is also used in other places referring to descendants, notably when God is speaking to Noah and Abram about His covenant:

[Genesis 9:8-9] [8] Then God spoke to Noah and to his sons with him, saying: [9] "And as for Me, behold, I establish My covenant with you and with your descendants [zera] after you, (NKJV) {notation added for clarification}

[Genesis 13:14-15] [14] And the Lord said to Abram, after Lot had separated from him: "Lift your eyes now and look from the place where you are—northward, southward, eastward, and westward; [15] for all the land which you see I give to you and your descendants [zera] forever. (NKJV) {notation added for clarification}

This "seed" of the serpent may not be limited to a metaphorical context only. I personally believe that the "seed" referenced here is a legitimate line of descendants from those who have practiced and taught separation from God as a condition and lifestyle. As with anything in the generations, if given enough time and with the right methods, you could breed in such a way as to get a 'pure' version of what is being sought after. This wouldn't be the first time in history that corrupted men have had delusional ideas regarding a purified race, or even eliminating an entire race as part of a method to achieve twisted beliefs that originate straight from the pits of hell.

It's only the first phase in advancing and developing a godless breed of person when you teach them all manner of evil and satanic rituals from birth with which to evict the Holy Spirit from a person's vessel, and reach a level of covenant and dedication to Satan that by all appearances is irreversible. But even with this, there is still a soul within, albeit completely bound and shattered. The next generation would be to modify human genetics, whereby many new and unprecedented possibilities come into play. Imagine the union of human flesh with cybernetics and augmentation? For example, in the pursuit of longevity, replacing a human heart with an artificial one along with liver, kidneys, and perhaps even parts of the brain? At what point does the human end and the machine begin? Within the scope of genetics, it is not impossible to alter the human brain in such a way as to suppress the regions of the brain that handle emotion, empathy, and conscience. To adapt the human mind to have a genetically seared conscience becomes a concern rather than a science fiction plot.

I am not anti-science or anti-medicine, but I pose the question: At what point does the flesh cease to live naturally, and the spirit is yielded back to God? If the line of death becomes blurred, and if natural life has ended but is prolonged artificially, what exactly are you coexisting with? When natural life has ended, the persons' spirit is given up and returns to God from whence it came – and the soul of that person crosses over into one of two possible destinations for eternity. Yet if the flesh and blood are artificially sustained, if the brain retains its functions of memory and operation without the spirit and soul of the individual, this opens a new can of worms. In my personal opinion, this would be a gut-wrenching nightmare of an opportunity for Satan to have a free vessel in which to operate – completely devoid of any restraint from the soul (the mind, will, and emotions) of that former person. Externally, I postulate that we may sense or feel a shift take place in that person when the God-given life has returned to its final destination – and we are left with merely an artificial after-image of that individual.

But to return on topic, I feel as though Satan could use genetics as he did once before to amass his seed and form the ranks of his army to fight against God's people and even the plans and purposes of God. It isn't too far from the imagination to take human embryos and breed super-soldiers through genetic alteration. Scientists have already done many things with humans and animals involving genetics, and that's only the things they publish and talk about. Take a look again at the description of the nightmarish creatures that ravage through this planet in the prophetic Scriptures about the end times. Yeah, God can snap His fingers and create horrible flying insect creatures like locusts that have human faces and hair like women but have the appearance of horses and pop their collars off to cut them loose on humanity – whereby people have heart attacks and die from total fear and horror. But consider also the effect of 'visual language representation' of two totally different time periods. Is it possible that these Scriptures could be describing genetically altered metahumans, that become so totally demon possessed that they are literally "living" and "breathing" extensions of Satan's seed?

At the risk of sounding awfully Terminator-ish here, I bring this back to biblical prophecy and text. Remember, "as things were in the days of Noah". You had the highest level of immorality, every forbidden act coming out into full view being widely accepted and practiced. Full-blown genetic mutation turned evil giants that weren't even born of God's Spirit against mankind and ate everything on the earth, killed people and animals, drank their blood, etc. "So shall it be at the coming of the Son of Man". In many ways, we are experiencing the beginning of the gross evil and deepest darkness. Many things once considered forbidden and taboo are now openly accepted and practiced. We now have the 'transhuman' movement in its beginning stages and is rapidly growing in popularity and advancement. This is the study and development of making humans potentially live longer, become smarter, stronger, faster, and even be modified at the genetic level to mitigate the limitations and effects of the natural lifespan and condition of man.

Who is to say they won't uncover the decedents of Anak and recreate their DNA within human embryos?

[Numbers 13:32b-33] [32b] They said, "The land we explored is one that devours those who live there. All the people we saw there are very tall. [33] We saw Nephilim there. (The descendants of Anak are Nephilim.) We felt as small as grasshoppers, and that's how we must have looked to them." (GW)

As the original Nephilim turned against each other in soulless blood battles to the death, in some ways their descendants inherited these traits, and that is what is meant by "the land devours those who live there". This was infighting amongst groups, a deadly habitat where the threat of treachery always loomed. Mind you, these Nephilim existed even after the flood as it was written in Scripture, "and also in the days after" (Genesis 6:4). Another warning from the book of Enoch tells us in regards to the Nephilim:

[Enoch 15:10] "They shall cause lamentation. No food shall they eat; and they shall be thirsty; they shall be concealed, and shall not rise up against the sons of men, and against women; for they come forth during the days of slaughter and destruction."

If it is true that they cause lamentation by oppressing and tormenting us, but beyond this are concealed until a predetermined day of slaughter and destruction – at which point they could inhabit corporeal vessels of genetically modified servants that are Satan's seed, it would stand to reason that this would be a possible candidate for a biblical end-time army that works together in unison to ravage anything in its wake.

The Nephilim have been concealed for a long time, although there have been many pieces of evidence and fossils from multitudes of discoveries having found skeletons 15 to 30 feet tall, molars the size of golf balls, large tools that proportionally would be used by someone 15 to 20 feet tall, etc. But this prophetic warning tells us that they will rise again in the end times, in the "days of slaughter and destruction." Is it not possible that these mighty warrior killing machines that have the biggest penchant for vengeance wouldn't be the ideal force of destruction to lay waste to a sin-filled land? Isn't that rather befitting of the statement towards their origin: "as in the days of Noah?" Let's look at one last Scripture, but I want to use this Scripture in its first, original translation from Hebrew to Greek which is known as the Septuagint:

[Isaiah 13:3] I give command, and I bring them: giants are coming to fulfil my wrath, rejoicing at the same time and insulting. (Brenton's Septuagint)

This in context is talking about the destruction of Babylon, in biblical times. But I believe this also has a near and far prophetic value as well when you zoom out to consider all things. Let's see this Scripture in a more modern translation than the original Septuagint:

[Isaiah 13:3] I have commanded my sanctified ones, I have also called my mighty ones for mine anger, even them that rejoice in my highness. (KJV)

Listen to what is being said from Barnes' Notes on the Bible:

I have commanded - This is the language of God in reference to those who were about to destroy Babylon. "He" claimed the control and direction of all their movements; and though the command was not understood by "them" as coming from Him, yet it was by His direction, and in accordance with His plan (compare the notes at Isaiah 10:7; Isaiah 45:5-6). The "command" was not given by the prophets, or by an audible voice; but it was His secret purpose and direction that led them to this enterprise.

In other words, God said He commanded them, but the army didn't know they were being commanded at all. The army thought it was doing its own thing, having its own way. There wasn't a prophet or an audible voice from Heaven telling them what to do – and yet they were playing right into God's sovereign plan the whole time.

my sanctified ones - The Medes and Persians; not called sanctified because they were holy, but because they were set apart by the divine intention and purpose to accomplish this. The word sanctify (קָדַשׁ qâdash) often means "to set apart" – either to God; to an office; to any sacred use; or to any purpose of religion, or of accomplishing any of the divine plans. Thus, it means to: "dedicate one to the office of priest" (Exodus 28:41); "to set apart or dedicate an altar" (Exodus 39:36); "to dedicate a people" (Exodus 19:10-14); "to appoint, or institute a fast" (Joel 1:14;

Joel 2:15); "to sanctify a war" (Joel 3:9), that is, to prepare one's-self for it, or make it ready. Here it means, that the Medes and Persians were set apart, in the purpose of God, to accomplish His designs in regard to Babylon (compare the note at Isaiah 10:5-6).

The Medes and Persians were hardly godly on a good day, and yet they were attributed as being sanctified ones. This is a breakdown of what the word 'sanctify' can mean in different contexts. When applied to people, it can have a different meaning than when applied to objects or actions.

my mighty ones - Those who are strong; and who are so entirely under My direction, that they may be called Mine.

For Mine anger - To accomplish the purposes of my anger against Babylon.

Even them that rejoice in My highness - It cannot be supposed that the Medes and Persians really exulted, or rejoiced in God or in His plans. The word rendered 'my highness' means, properly, "my majesty," or "glory." When applied to people, as it often is, it means pride or arrogance. It means here, the high and exalted plan of God in regard to Babylon. It was a mighty undertaking; and one in which the power, the justice, and the dominion of God over nations would be evinced. In accomplishing this, the Medes and Persians would rejoice or exult, not as the fulfilling of the plan of God; but they would exult as if it were their own plan, though it would be really the glorious plan of God. Wicked people often exult in their success; they glory in the execution of their purposes; but they are really accomplishing the plans of God, and executing His great designs.

When many of us, including myself before I had studied this, hear the word "sanctified" we tend to automatically think of synonyms such as: pure, holy, righteous. While it is true these can describe parts of sanctification, the term itself is better defined as: 'to set apart for special use or purpose.' It is entirely possible for God to *sanctify* a nation of sinners as a vengeful army, to use against another nation or people, so long as it executes the will of God or the judgment of God, particularly to fulfill Scripture. This wouldn't be the first time God has done this either, as other Scripture points out that God is likened to a blacksmith that creates weapons fit for their work, and names Himself as the One who creates the destroyer to destroy. Additionally, and perhaps more directly, other Scripture reveals that God is the one who raised up the ruthless Babylonians who would go out and destroy in accordance with God's judgment.

Regardless of whether or not Nephilim are returning to fulfill prophetic destruction across the land, or even whether or not Satan will attempt to use forbidden technologies to corrupt and pollute a portion of human DNA once again to create vessels which he can operate through in a sickening mockery of God's ways, one thing is clear. We are living on the edge of the times, and the days ahead are only going to get darker in terms of the prophetic biblical timeline. God provides us many counterparts to these prophetic warnings and insights – the keys to victory, and how to overcome this darkness with the Light of His glory.

I have been saying that it is about a deep, intimate, personal relationship with God. Religion is a stale piece of bread, and it won't make the cut. Being involved in a two-way love relationship with God the Father, Jesus the Son, and the Holy Spirit of God is the only way to stay close enough to the Fire that you hear His still, small voice. In this way, you will know whether to turn to the left or the right in times of trouble or need. With a foundation of love, which God Himself is – you can discern the moving of the Spirit and follow His leadership accordingly. What works for you may not work for someone else, and what works for another may not work for you. We must keep our eyes on Jesus and follow Him in the unique ways He tells us in our hearts because God has different plans and purposes for each one of us; but no matter what way God speaks to you, everything He says and does will always line up with His Word.

THE TRUTH OF
GHOSTS

I would like to start this out upfront by saying that there are several different ways in which people interpret the term 'ghosts' and have different points of view on what a ghost actually is, or isn't. In terms of a ghost being the disembodied spirit of a human who has been deceased, but still roams the earth for any reason or purpose – this in fact is not possible. However, this doesn't conclude the matter – there are other explanations as to why apparitions and ghosts can manifest themselves, appear as human beings, have the likeness and memories of individuals, and even move objects. The Bible tells us why a ghost cannot be a human spirit roaming the earth, whether because it has unfinished business, or somehow was lost or unable to transition into the next life:

[Job 7:9-10] ⁹ As the cloud disappears and vanishes away, So he who goes down to the grave does not come up. [10] He shall never return to his house, Nor shall his place know him anymore. (NKJV)

[Hebrews 9:27] And as it is appointed for men to die once, but after this the judgment, (NKJV)

[Psalm 146:4] When his breath departs, he returns to the earth; on that very day his plans perish. (ESV)

The Bible, when read altogether in context, explains to us that when a person dies their spirit and soul leave their body and immediately goes to be judged to determine where they will spend eternity in either one of two places – Heaven or hell. There is no other place and no in-between (Luke 16:19-31).

Having established the fact that human spirits cannot speak or return from their eternal destination, there are some other spiritual forces at work that can mimic this perceived reality. We know that Satan's main goal is to deceive people quite literally by any means necessary – to steal them away from the truth and thus away from God, to torment their souls in hell forever. Whatever it takes to accomplish this purpose, even if it requires him or his demonic host to divulge truth and speak kindly, so be it:

[2 Corinthians 11:14-15] [14] And no wonder! For Satan himself transforms himself into an angel of light. [15] Therefore it is no great thing if his ministers also transform themselves into ministers of righteousness, whose end will be according to their works. (NKJV)

I think many of us have been in those types of relationships where everything seems maybe a little to-good-to-be-true in the beginning, or at least that our partner was exceeding our expectations consistently for some time. And as things developed and became more serious, we may have felt comfortable and let our guard down and perhaps committed to things that placed us in vulnerable positions, relying on trust to stay the course. And that's when the proverbial monster came out of the closet and showed its true nature, oftentimes when it was too late for us to turn back at that point. What we were then left with was a very shattered heart full of self-loathing and bitterness, and a warped mindset that believes we somehow deserve to be in this pit, based on the gaslighting and lies fed to us every day through abuse.

If mere men and women are capable of doing this to one another, how much more Satan and his demonic hosts? If the best way to deceive a person into the pits of hell is by causing them to believe a ghost is their deceased relative, why not put on a show and reinforce the lie over a given time period? The ghost itself, pretending to be their deceased mother, for example, could say there is no Heaven or hell – and offer guidance and instruction in how to reach the 'afterlife' so they could be reunited forever. This is an example of how a demon can masquerade as a ghost for the ultimate purpose of realizing one more soul being stolen away from God.

The only kind of disembodied spirits that will ever be found on this earth are those evil spirits (demons) that came out of the Nephilim when they died – and they are evil, through and through. They aren't just mindless brutes that are always offensive – they operate out of pride, revenge, and deception. They have supernatural power as well as intellect, and they have had thousands of years to study the psyche of humans. If you take a step back and do the math here, you would be wise to be on guard against them knowing that their abilities far surpass those of our flesh in every way. We should have a healthy understanding that we alone are outmatched and easily defeated, and that only through the shed blood of Jesus Christ are we victorious.

Separate from disembodied spirits, we have a fringe explanation that involves the fragmentation of the human soul, which is partially or wholly demon-possessed. I am referring to a phenomenon known as "soul invasion". Now to fully understand this problem and realize how this is affecting us, we need to first understand what the soul is and how it affects us:

[Genesis 2:7] And the Lord God formed man of the dust of the ground, and breathed into his nostrils the breath of life; and man became a living soul. (KJV)

Our soul is our mind, will, and emotions. How we think, the things we choose, and how we feel all comes from our soul. This is a major part of who we are. Our logic, judgment, reasoning, and any other faculty of the mind are usually dependent upon the condition of our soul. Even our desires and impulses are rooted in the nature of the soul. Each emotion we experience is deeply woven throughout the soul nature.

This is why born-again Christians can still be demon-possessed. Upon receiving Christ into our heart and believing in Him, our *spirit-man* is perfected and resurrected to life in Christ. The Holy Spirit now abides and lives within our renewed spirit, and the devil has no grounds there. This is the proverbial 'temple' the Spirit now dwells within, inside of us. The soul and body, however, are not instantly perfected upon receiving Christ. If it were so, then all our thoughts and emotions and memories would be instantly purged and pure, and never again would an evil thought come across our mind – sin would have no place in our thoughts and feelings, and our bodies would be perfected and made whole instantly. Unfortunately, this is not the case. The soul and body are still bound and it requires healing and deliverance, righteous living, and obedience to God to see the *sanctification process* through. This is a process that takes our lifetime to persist in. This is why the enemy targets the soul and seeks to possess it – because it is the seat of all fleshly lusts, desires, and appetites:

[1 Peter 2:11] Dear friends, I urge you, as foreigners and exiles, to abstain from sinful desires, which wage war against your soul. (NIV)

We can see here from this Scripture that the battle takes place and wars against the soul of a person. We can glean from this that the nature of our soul is vulnerable and very pliable in the sense that many functions of our soul can be affected by our surroundings. In other words, our souls are very fragile and delicate and must be guarded and protected seriously every day.

The enemy loves to operate within and against the soul of a person because he can appeal to the affections and emotions of a person with common ground. In other words, the evil nature of the enemy has common ground with the corrupt, fallen nature of our flesh. This is like two magnets clicking together and it's hard to separate them. The enemy's lies and desires are attracted to the untransformed soul nature of a person. The enemy knows full well that he could dominate the physical and soul-nature of a person. His limitation is his powerlessness over the born-again Spirit of a believer in Christ.

That is why the enemy does not care if a person goes to a church where the Spirit of God is not evident or welcomed. His greatest fear is a person's spirit coming into contact with the Holy Spirit of God. He knows we are creatures of emotion and it doesn't matter if we tear up in church or are stirred up with hype – as long as God's Holy Spirit is not touching our spirit-man and changing the heart.

The soul shares a seat of power with the heart concerning the passions, feelings, and desires of a person. Those things that we want, strive for, and believe in are a matter of the soul as well. God intended that each person have one soul with which to love and serve God. However, the Bible gives us an example of how a person can have more than one soul:

[James 1:8] being a double-minded man, unstable and restless in all his ways [in everything he thinks, feels, or decides]. (AMP)

The original Greek word for double-minded is dipsuchos, meaning "a person with two souls."

Strongs 1374: dípsyxos (an adjective, derived from 1364 /dís, "two" and 5590 /psyxḗ, "soul") – properly, "two souled"; (figuratively) "double-minded," i.e. a person "split in half," vacillating like a "spiritual schizophrenic."

Interestingly enough this word occurs only in the book of James, and once at that. He breaks this down to explain the woes, symptoms, and signs of a double-minded person. He says essentially that a double-minded person is confused in their thoughts, actions, and feelings. In other words, their mind, will, and emotions. This is saying that a double-minded person has two or more souls residing within. One fights and resists the other, and such an afflicted person is at war with themselves in all that they do. Such a person is so torn by an inner conflict that they cannot ever lean with confidence on God or His gracious promises. James tells us that such a person is unstable in all they do. This is similar to a drunken person who cannot walk in a straight line.

This doesn't automatically imply that the other soul parts are foreign, or invading. Countless times we have seen within deliverance and exorcism sessions that just regular, everyday life that is often filled with hurtful and traumatic experiences is more than enough to shatter, fracture, split, or otherwise cause fragmented soul parts within a person's mind. Now, the person may also be unaware that there is an internal conflict and struggle. It could also be that multiple souls are not necessarily at war with one another, either. We have seen situations where multiple soul fragments simply exist inside of a person – unaware that they are trapped inside a vessel. They might surface unknowingly in certain situations and circumstances – and cause stress or grief that is unattributed to any cause.

At times, we have witnessed individuals behave normally until a small change has taken place in their surroundings, whether it be a person, a place, an object that had some kind of childhood attachment, or even a familiar smell, which triggered a very wounded soul fragment that was possessed with a spirit of fear – and it manifested in that person and completely changed their actions and behavior according to the wounds of the fragment and the types of demonic spirits seeking to influence it. In almost all of those cases, we were no longer dealing with the person sitting in front of us, but rather the 8-year old version of them that suffered the original trauma that was scared and hurt, willing to defend itself at any cost, for example.

Remember the soul is the mind, will, and emotions of a person. This simply means that a person could experience thoughts running across their mind that they would otherwise have no business thinking about. It could be that a person suffers from, or experiences emotions that surface without any apparent reason – and the person is left wondering where these emotions are coming from and why they are feeling them. It also includes decisions and choices – where a person looks back in hindsight and wonders why on earth, they have just done something or said something that they would otherwise not normally do. Oftentimes, behavior and actions that are out of character for a person can be rooted in the inner influence of soul parts that are wounded, out of place, not their own, etc. Many of these soul fragments can be invaded or influenced by demonic spirits as well. There is a process within deliverance and exorcism that brings up these soul fragments, ministers to them, casts the demons out of them, and removes their legal rights – while the Holy Spirit provides healing and restoration to those fragmented parts of the soul. Either God can take them, or safely reintegrate them back into the core of that person.

Also, keep in mind that not every traumatic experience is a soul fragment that needs to be removed entirely. Sometimes, God has permitted certain things into our lives because that is part of our testimony that we will use to bring others to Christ.

You will know when healing is required because your testimony should be something that can be discussed without reservation of pain, bitterness, unforgiveness, or any other ungodly feeling that demons could use to infiltrate.

Now that we have a foundation of what the soul of a person is and what some of its functions are, we need to expand into the next layer of *soul invasion*. What we will learn about now is how two or more souls can link and connect with one another. We call this connection between two people's souls a 'soul tie'. Soul ties can be godly, or ungodly. And soul ties are found in the Bible.

One example of a godly soul tie is in a godly marriage. In this case, God links the two together and the Bible tells us that they become one flesh. As a result of them becoming one flesh, it binds them together and they uniquely cleave unto one another. The purpose of this cleaving together is to build a very healthy, strong, and close relationship between a man and a woman.

[Matthew 19:5] … 'For this reason a man shall leave his father and mother and shall be joined inseparably to his wife, and the two shall become one flesh' … (AMP)

Soul ties can also be found in close or strong friendships – they are not just limited to a marriage, as we can see from David and Jonathan:

[1 Samuel 18:1] When David had finished speaking to Saul, the soul of Jonathan was bonded to the soul of David, and Jonathan loved him as himself. (AMP)

So, we see here from Scripture that soul ties are real, are not limited to the marriage covenant, and can be Godly in purpose. However, there can be negative effects from soul ties and this is what we call ungodly soul ties. Biblically, we see an ungodly soul tie formed through an act of defilement:

[Genesis 34:2-3] 2 When … the son of Hamor … saw her, he kidnapped her and lay [intimately] with her by force [humbling and offending her]. 3 But his soul longed for and clung to Dinah daughter of Jacob, and he loved the girl and spoke comfortingly to her young heart's wishes. (AMP)

This is why it has been known for a person to still have 'feelings' towards an ex-lover or former sexual partner that they have no right to be attracted to in that way. Even 20 years down the road, a person might still think of that particular lover – even if they are across the country and have their own family. All because of a soul tie, and the things being transferred through that link. When two or more souls connect, the soul-nature of those people can pass between each person in both directions, through the soul tie. This will affect the composition of one's soul in the short-term and long-term, and these types of things need to be cast out and cleansed from within.

There can be an accumulation of thoughts, feelings, and emotions from a particular person being transferred into another person over time that can develop into an invading consciousness that is not your own. Demons can also utilize and take advantage of ungodly soul ties, and use them to transfer spirits from one person to another. We have seen in deliverance sessions where demonic attacks were stopped completely by simply severing a soul tie. Soul ties can also be formed through vows, commitments, and agreements. Vows are known to bind the soul (Numbers 30:2), and marriage itself consists of vows and binds the two together (Ephesians 5:31).

Therefore, it stands to reason that agreements, vows, and commitments are valid methods of creating soul ties. This is why we are always admonished to be careful what we are agreeing with. This is also why it is important to beware that we are not unequally yoked:

[2 Corinthians 6:14] Do not be unequally bound together with unbelievers [do not make mismatched alliances with them, inconsistent with your faith]. For what partnership can righteousness have with lawlessness? Or what fellowship can light have with darkness? (AMP)

This is not saying ignore and separate ourselves from unbelievers or those who are bound. Jesus didn't do that; in fact, he sat down and ate together with tax collectors and sinners. Or in today's terms, some politicians and bankers. This is directly telling us to be aware and cautious of what agreements and commitments we are making with those who do not match our realm of belief. The Scripture is essentially warning us to be careful of making ungodly soul ties that might cause us to act contrary to our faith, or have to violate God's word to fulfill the desires of those who follow the world.

Soul *invasion* is a part of another person's conscience (mind, will, and emotions) transferring through a soul tie into your own soul. That person whose soul is invading may not even be aware that they are residing within another vessel. We can't hold the people responsible for these kinds of things because this is a spiritual problem. The main thing that happens is we become somewhat clouded internally because our brains are trying to process multiple thoughts, feelings, and emotions. Others around us might experience these changes or shifts in behavior. Even if not, we may struggle internally with confusion and difficulty. A simpler way of putting it is that if we are afflicted with soul invasion, we may even have foreign and misleading 'intuition' or 'gut feelings' that are not entirely genuine – and this could cause confusion; hence being unstable in all of our ways, as James described in the Bible.

The following is a testimony of deliverance we did a few years ago with two different people and their cases of soul invasion:

"AMAZING! HERE IN RECENT DAYS, THE LORD HAS BEEN DEALING WITH US CONCERNING SOUL INVASION AND THE DEEP IMPORTANCE OF UPROOTING THESE EXTRA-CONSCIOUS FRAGMENTS OF OTHERS' SOULS.

TODAY WE WORKED ON TWO PEOPLE THAT HAD JUST SUCH A DILEMMA. YEARS OF TEENAGE TRAUMA PRODUCED A 'LONGING FOR BELONGING' WHICH RESULTED IN A DEEP STRIVING TO ADOPT THE CHARACTERISTICS AND PERSONALITIES OF OTHERS. UNFORTUNATELY, THESE ALL CREATED SOUL TIES WITH THOSE PEOPLE WHICH THEN TRANSFERRED SOUL INVADERS AND EVEN DEMONS FROM THEM!

AS THE ANOINTING INCREASED AND WE SOUGHT THE LORD, MANY SOUL INVADERS SURFACED WITHIN THEM AND AS THEIR NAMES WERE CALLED OUT, THEY HAD TO DEPART AND RETURN TO JESUS FOR GOING BACK TO WHERE THEY BELONG. WHEN THE LORD DIRECTED US TO CUT OFF AND

SEPARATE THE MEMORIES AND PAST EXPERIENCES OF THE SOUL INVADERS OFF OF THE MEMORIES AND PAST EXPERIENCES OF THE PERSON BEING WORKED ON, THE SOUL INVADER BECAME FURIOUS AND DEPARTED WITH VENGEFUL DAGGERS COMING OUT OF HIS EYES!

I BELIEVE THAT SOME INVADERS HAVE A PURPOSE - PERHAPS A VOID WITHIN THEM THAT THEY ARE FILLING BY 'LIVING INSIDE' OF SOMEONE ELSE, ATTACHING THEIR SOUL CONSCIOUSNESS TO THE MEMORIES AND EXPERIENCES OF OTHERS. WHEN THIS FANTASY IS DISRUPTED, THEY BECOME ANGRY AND WANT TO ACT OUT.

WHAT'S MORE THAN THAT IS WE ENCOUNTERED ANIMAL INVADERS WITHIN THEM! ACTUAL FRAGMENTS OF PETS THAT HAD INVADED THEM THROUGH SOUL TIES. AS WE CAST OUT THE INVADING SOUL PARTS OF THE ANIMALS (WHICH WERE CATS) THE MOST INCREDIBLE SUPERNATURAL THING HAPPENED. TWO ACTUAL

CATS APPEARED RIGHT OUTSIDE THE FRONT DOOR JUST SITTING THERE STARING AT THE PEOPLE BEING DELIVERED. THEY WOULDN'T MOVE FOR ANYTHING! IN FACT, THEY ONLY DEPARTED WHEN THE DELIVERANCE HAD BEEN COMPLETED.

I FIRMLY BELIEVE THAT THE TRUTH OF SOUL INVASION IS DEEP AND REAL AND THAT ANIMALS ARE NOT EXCLUDED FROM SOUL INVASION OR TRANSFERENCE THROUGH SOUL TIES. THIS TOPIC REQUIRES MUCH MORE INVESTIGATION AND STUDY."

In the above testimony, this person was very close to their pets. A soul tie was formed between the owner and the pet, and since that pet had died, this person was carrying a part of that cat 'alive' within them – and this could have established some unhealthy grounds for the enemy to potentially work with. The purpose is that we should have wholeness, soundness, and no extra parts of anyone or anything else inside of us except what God specifically ordains.

In another session we did with a married couple, Bob and Jen, there was an evil soul invader of a witch that possessed their friend Ana from church. They could both feel some strange activity in the spirit realm coming from Ana but could not pinpoint it. Jen backed off from the relationship towards Ana, and Ana could sense this, so she started texting and talking to the husband Bob without his wife knowing.

Because Bob engaged in this, a door was opened and the evil witch used this opportunity to inject a soul fragment of Ana into Bob! If Bob had included his wife and discussed having a conversation with Ana together with Jen, they could have both agreed not to do so given the situation through prayer – and the devil would have no legal right to enter Bob. Now the witch could control the soul fragment of Ana within Bob to severely influence him by proxy. This is why it is so important to {in most cases, where possible} minister men-to-men and women-to-women or married couples together ministering to others. Two-by-two accountability is a very important protective measure.

Once the soul invader of Ana was cast out of Bob and the witchcraft dealt with, it was less than one week before Ana herself showed up for deliverance! No one had said anything to her, because of the awkwardness of the situation. She came led by the Spirit to be delivered! When she was worked on, among some other things, one of the problems was that she was possessed by an evil soul invader of a witch. This too was removed and she walks in freedom from that bondage to this day.

It was amazing that all of this transpired without anyone saying anything. This proves that to deal with a lot of the issues of life – we must attack what is happening in the spirit realm FIRST. Then, things will unfold accordingly in the natural realm. We should always be seeking God for what is taking place in the spirit realm and then address the issues there

BEFORE we go and do anything in the natural realm (as the Lord directs and leads).

Not every fragmented soul part or soul invader is limited to occupying a human or animal, either. It is entirely possible within the scope and boundary of the supernatural and the spirit realm that such things may exist in places or regions as well. Much the same as evil spirits, demons, and the fallen angels exist in places and over entire regions. This helps explain why 'ghosts' can be seen in various places where no corporeal lifeform is present.

Remember, soul fragments are strictly the mind, will, and emotions of a person. Because of the way God created the human soul, by breathing the breath of life into the nostrils, the very core of a soul comes from God. As humans, we have the free will to choose whether our soul nature will cleave to the goodness of God or the ways of the world. Therefore, demons can usurp and inhabit fragments of a human soul and thus influence it directly through pain, wounds, trauma, and sin. In other words, when looking upon a 'ghost' you may see the real form and shape of the human it is representing. This is possible because the soul fragment may know who it is and what it looks like, the information contained within the thoughts and memories of the fragment. The demon can hijack this fragment and use its supernatural power to manifest itself and appear as the fragment indicates from its thoughts and memories. 'Ghosts' can speak in the same voice, pitch, and tone while having the memories and personality traits unique to the person it is portraying. In every way, it can be entirely convincing – unless it says or does something that contradicts the Word of God.

There are so many variables that it is impossible to cover them all. Ghosts could appear genuine, say and do good things, even help children and provide wisdom that leads to success. But what type of entity is behind it? What type of rank or function does that entity possess? What level of authority does that entity have in the spiritual realm, and what is the end goal, or does it even have one? Is a well-meaning human soul fragment possessed by a weaker spirit whose function is inordinate affection? Idol worship – and you are the idol?

But let me ask you the all-important question: When is the last time you heard of a ghost ministering salvation to a person and leading them to Jesus Christ?

Now I will say this if you are the type of person who has had an encounter with what appeared to be a 'ghost' as far as your mind could wrap around the visitation experience – and you can't find anything wrong or demonic about it, to the point that none of the experience contradicts the Word of God, then perhaps you had a genuine angelic encounter. There are many testimonies that God has sent angels to look and appear like deceased relatives, and has spoken to people while in these forms, for varying purposes. To save them from trouble, to prevent disaster or death, or to warn and otherwise guide them. Simply put, these are holy angels only appearing as people familiar to us to get our attention or cause us to adhere to the moment and receive the purpose of the visitation. In any case, there should be an atmosphere of peace and love that accompanies anything that comes from Heaven. A deep knowing within the heart and spirit of a person that true, total love is behind every action. If this is not the case, I would personally pray and ask for more discernment, not wanting to be deceived.

Perhaps one of the clearest illustrations in the Bible about how a disembodied human spirit cannot possibly communicate with other humans in the world of the living is that of Lazarus and the rich man, which can be read in full in Luke 16:19-31.

THE
SUMMARY

We have covered a lot in this book, and there is a lot to digest within these topics. As I had said in the beginning, I ask that you pray the Holy Spirit to enlighten you to all wisdom that leads into truth, and to allow the Spirit of God to give you wisdom in all things as it pertains to your walk with God.

Let's review a summarization of what we have learned so far:

We have three major events to understand:

1. The Fall of Lucifer, and a third of the angels.
2. The Fall of the Holy Watchers, and the rise of the Nephilim.
3. The origin of evil spirits upon the earth, and the return of the Nephilim.

- Satan and the third of the angels he convinced to join him are currently and actively fighting against us. These entities comprise the ranks and hierarchy of hell. They abide and operate as the hosts of wickedness in spiritual places, as there is no longer any place found for them in Heaven (the third Heaven, and above).

- Their present location of operations consists of the first- and second-heavens, which are the powers of the air (above our planet) and within the known universe (which is considered the second-heaven).

- The original third of the angelic host that rebelled with Lucifer is not strictly limited to only dwelling in heavenly places. The Bible says they were cast down to the earth, with Satan. Dependent upon the assignments of hell, it is entirely possible and at times likely that high-ranking demonic forces can roam the earth and possess individuals if it supported the advancement of their kingdom.

- There is also no evidence to suggest that these
upper-echelon fallen angels aren't able to
communicate with and traverse through any part
of the spirit realm, including hell, and return to
their assigned posts to carry out assignments. The
Bible simply states that "no longer was any place
found in Heaven for him [the dragon; Satan] and
his angels." This, in conjunction with the fact that
Satan came and appeared before God in Heaven
with a group of other angels. God permitted his
entrance into Heaven and his audience before the
Throne, where God offered Job into Satan's
hands. Second also, during a dialogue regarding
king Ahab, the prophet Micaiah son of Imlah,
explained a vision he had in which God was upon
His throne, asking the holy angels who among
them would convince king Ahab to go to his
death at Ramoth-Gilead? A spirit {notably not a
'Son of God' or 'holy angel'} came forward and
offered to become a lying spirit in the mouths of

all the prophets, to deceive the king into attending a battle which would surely end his life. God permitted this and sent that spirit forth to accomplish its works.

- The third of the angels are known to be referred to as "fallen angels" since they fell with Lucifer in the earliest known stage of rebellion. The spiritual destination of torment for those who rebel against God, known as hell, was created for the devil and his angels. This is their assigned judgment preceding the final judgment in the lake of fire, where hell itself will be thrown into on the final day.

- Unlike condemned demonic spirits in hell, who can enter or exit to fulfill assignments given them by Satan, the lake of fire is inescapable and all who are banished to it will remain for eternity. Eventually, every type and class of created lifeform specific to angelic and human entities, whose names are not written in the book of life –

or angels who have sinned in any capacity, will be condemned to the lake of fire.

- The Holy Watchers from Genesis 6 are also known to be referred to as "fallen angels" because they too, like the original third, were once holy. The Watchers' sin was when they acted out their premeditated plan to deny their dwelling in Heaven and procreate with human women upon the earth, and setting in motion the chain of events that led to the flood in Noah's time.

- "The Watchers" as they are most commonly referred to after their fall, are not actively fighting against us because they are forever bound within the abyss until the final day. There are references contained within the book of Enoch to suggest there were approximately 200 angels that made up the Watchers of Genesis 6.

- What are referred to as evil spirits, demons, familiar spirits, bad ghosts, etc. are the disembodied spirits that proceeded from the flesh of the Nephilim when they died, as was spoken of in the book of Enoch. The term "demon" is used generically by many to refer to an "evil" entity. Here we are trying to be more precise with our usage of the word to encompass *the evil spirits that proceeded from the Nephilim.*

- The Bible never uses the term "fallen angels" so there is no true differentiation between what is called a 'fallen angel' and a 'demon'. In essence, you could classify all of them as one or the other. All angels that sinned have fallen, and all of them that fell have become demons. Even the demons that came from the Nephilim are simply the offspring of demons, during their fathers' transition from holy angels to fallen angels due to their sin involving human women. The differences between them are found in when they fell, why they fell, and how they war against us today.

- It is important to note that the terms used to describe spiritual forces can vary significantly throughout each system of belief, across many denominations, and even differ according to different regions, social, or cultural barriers. It is unwise to argue the definitive terms, but rather to show the differences in function and assignment, rank and authority. Whether we are referencing demons, fallen angels, or evil spirits – they are all of the same origins in the context of spiritual beings. Some rebelled first, others later, and some were manifested as a result of rebellion. Some dwell in high and lofty places, others under the earth, still more operate on the earth, and some are bound to where they cannot operate at all.

If you read the book of Enoch, the Watchers petitioned Enoch to intercede for them after God judged them for their sin. God already told Enoch they would never find peace or rest – but Enoch obliged the Watchers and interceded for them anyway. He wrote a petition and presented it to God in prayer until he fell asleep. While dreaming, God took him into Heaven and spoke to him among many things, one of which God said to Enoch, "Tell the Watchers that it should be them who intercedes for man – and not man for them."

God did not change His mind and kept the judgment in place. They could only look on in torment as their offspring fell by the sword. We also learn here that not all beings born into this world are born of the Spirit of God. The Nephilim were created by the spirits of angels and women – therefore their spirits were evil and were fated to roam the earth, as the earth became their first estate.

This concludes our study on the initial fall of Lucifer, the fall of the Watchers, and the difference between fallen angels and demons.

Our society will always have a wide range of diverse individuals, and there will always be differences between us at some level. This is the beauty of individuality, and is a healthy example of each person's uniqueness in which we should embrace as a positive quality with respect. Not everyone will share the same belief or place the same value of importance upon a given topic, and it is each person's right to do so with their free will.

There will be individuals that either do not believe, or believe partially, in the ideals you have or in the faith you practice. It is entirely possible that people may reject the very contents of this book you have just read, or any other information that you have obtained throughout your journey of faith.

In these situations, I have only one admonishment: please do not argue the Word of God with anyone. In my personal experience, when people challenge and argue God's word, it is really a demonic force within them resisting the truth. If we engage in that battle in our flesh – we will lose. If the Holy Spirit isn't directing you to say or do anything, then don't.

The Word of God is pure, plain, and simple. It has true life in it by itself, and our job is to give that Word and let the people do with it what they may. It is not your job to make someone get saved, because you are not the Holy Spirit. We are supposed to live the Word by example and teach it, so people can see we live what we teach, and that by itself contains an anointing to reach a person's heart. If you're not living it at home, at work, and in church then don't teach it. You will be judged by God for that. The world has enough hypocrites that have many faces, but what they don't have is something genuine and true that isn't self-seeking.

If you are reviled and rejected after sharing a truth, don't entertain it. Just shake the dust off your feet and continue to love that person right where they are at. It's not the end. Silently pray for them in your quiet time, and then release them into God's hands. Let it go. There are so many other people that need to see and hear the love of God, this should be your focus.

I hope and pray that the contents of this book may enlighten you, and draw you closer to God in a deeper intimate relationship. I pray that the principles of spiritual warfare would be made known to you in a deeper way than before, and that you may fight spiritual battles with the Holy Spirit with clarity and precision. Thank you, and God bless.

www.ingramcontent.com/pod-product-compliance
Lightning Source LLC
Chambersburg PA
CBHW072021040426
42447CB00009B/1685